A LIFE ON THE TILES

Gareth Pugh

Copyright © Gareth Pugh 2024
All rights reserved.

Print ISBN 978-1-0687077-5-9

The right of Gareth Pugh to be identified as the author of this work has been asserted by him in accordance with the Copyright Designs and Patents Act 1988

No part of this publication may be reproduced, stored in a retrieval system, or transmitted in any form or by any means without the prior permission in writing of the publisher. Nor be otherwise circulated in any form or binding or cover other than that in which it is published and without a similar condition being imposed on the subsequent purchaser.

Published by
Llyfrau Cambria Books, Wales, United Kingdom.
Cambria Books and Cambria Stories are imprints of Cambria Publishing Ltd.
Discover our other books at: www.cambriabooks.co.uk

Chapters

1. In a cafe with Blue Nuns.	1
2. Woodworking and the YMCA.	11
3. Mitching School and Bird Nesting	16
4. Being an ATC cadet and Pop bottle refunds.	20
5. When Steptoe called into the Rose and Crown.	26
6. Roofing with a Lada Car.	41
7. "Let's play darts..."	53
8. Hooked on Fishing.	62
9. The African Trip.	70
10. Wood Turning.	77

1. In a cafe with Blue Nuns.

Rabaiottis Cafe in Pontypridd in the 1950s

THE year 1953 saw the coronation of Queen Elizabeth 11, author Ian Fleming publishing *Casino Royale* and the first instalment of the BBC's *The Good Old Days* screened on television.

Meanwhile there was a major event in Pontypridd when a baby boy named Gareth Pugh entered the world.

Gareth was born in Sycamore Street, Rhydyfelin, to proud parents Arthur and Lilian.

"I can remember my mother telling me that two girls used to push me around in a pram. There was one occasion when for some reason the pram went careering down a hill in Rhydyfelin and while doing so a lorry just missed poor old me in the pram.

"Naturally the two girls were very upset about it.

"My mother said it was a traumatic experience for them and not me because I was only a baby in a pram."

Gareth's standout memory of attending Rhydyfelin Infants School was bedding down for a sleep.

"At some time, probably in the afternoon, I along with the other children used to lay down on camp beds to have a sleep.

"How incredible was that?"

In 1957, Cardiff born singer Shirley Bassey had her first chart single with *The Banana Boat Song* while Brecon Beacons became the third of Wales's national parks.

It was also the year that Gareth, who was aged four, was part of the Pugh family which moved to Gas Road in Pontypridd, or Gas Lane as it was sometimes called, where they started a new family life in a flat above a butcher's shop.

Gareth said: "I can well remember that where we lived in Gas Lane there was a garden which backed on to a river.

"For me to get to the back garden my father, who had been in the Navy, made a ladder out of rope and wooden rungs because I found it difficult to negotiate.

"I loved being on that ladder and one day a neighbour's lad gave me a wooden sword.

"So, with sword in hand I used to climb down the ladder and get to a disused shed in the garden where I would smack rats with my sword. Another memory I have is playing with what I called black sand but was actually coal dust which used to come from the River Taff."

Back in the late 1950s Gareth loved the outdoor life and sitting at home watching a black and white television set really didn't interest him.

He said: "I wasn't interested in the news. I just couldn't be bothered with it

"The only TV programmes I watched back then were the ones showing *Popeye the Sailor.*

Popeye the Sailor was an American cartoon that was released between the years 1960 and 1963 with 220 episodes being produced.

It was while Gareth was watching *Popeye* one day there was a loud banging on the front door of his home.

"Suddenly my father grabbed me and my elder brother Gwyn under each arm and rushed out of the front door.

"We couldn't believe what was happening.

"I suppose we were confused and frightened because we did not know what was going on."

This was because there was a fire in the nearby Cold Stores which was very dangerous because it was close to a gasometer.

Gareth said: "If that fire had reached the gasometer it would have flattened Ponty.

"There were five fire engines there and all hell was breaking loose.

"My dad was a fireman, and he was helping as much as he could while my mother was making tea for everybody.

"As for me I, don't ask me why but when they got the fire under control, I got my wigwam and just sat in it.

"I think I had a picture taken which was published in the *Pontypridd Observer* newspaper".

Then there were days that if Gareth's behaviour was good his mother would take him on a shopping trip to Pontypridd where he was always on the lookout for biscuits.

He said: "There was one shop where they used to have biscuits on display about my height in square tins and of course I always had my eye on my favourites which were fig rolls."

And when Gareth wasn't eating fig rolls, he would be given a friction toy to play with.

Gareth(right) is pictured with his brothers Gwyn and Berwyn.

Friction toys were so named because they relied on an internal friction wheel that, when the toy was pulled backward built-up inertia to power the toy forward.

Gareth said: "Friction toys in the shape of cars or what have you were popular back then and of course after playing with them I used to take the friction wheel out."

Then there was a time that Gareth offered to help his neighbour dig his garden.

"Anyway, I grabbed a fork and decided to give it a go.

"I had red wellington boots on and when I plunged the fork into what I thought was the ground actually went through my welly and into my foot. I ended up with a welly full of blood.

"My mother sent for a doctor and thank goodness he arrived very quickly.

"The funny thing is that I only started crying when I saw the doctor".

Gareth's grandad Fred Pugh, lived in Thurston Rd, Trallwn, which was originally Rickard Terrace. When the Pugh family moved to Thurston Road, Gareth, who was aged seven, attended Coedpenmaen Junior School.

Gareth has special memories of a teacher there called Gomer Evans who he recalls as being 'tall and nice.'

"In one of my lessons I needed to paint a green field but instead of painting it simply green I used a mixture of green colours which when he saw it really impressed Mr Evans.

"He said that you could never get a field perfectly green, but he thought it was very clever and made quite a fuss of me. It was something I will never forget".

In 1964 Welsh actor Richard Burton married Elizabeth Taylor (for the first time) another Welsh born actor Victor Spinetti appeared with the Beatles in the film "A hard day's Night".

It was also the year Gareth Pugh failed the 11 plus exam.

Introduced in 1944, the 11 Plus examination was used to determine which type of school the student should attend. Gareth remembers that his dad was furious over the fact that I had failed the exam.

"He had passed the 11 Plus and had been a pupil at a Grammar School and he expected me do to the same".

So instead of going to Pontypridd Grammar School Gareth sat behind a desk at Coedylan Comprehensive School in Tyfica Road.

Pictured are Coedyland Comprehensive school pupils.

Fourth Row- *Billy Shevel, Kerry Mcfarlen, David Newbury, John Mitchell, Michael Davies, Angela Balchin, and Anne Allan.*

Third Row- *Eurfron Jones, Rosalyn Phipps, Keith Harris, Russel Davies, Gareth Ryan, Carol Evans, Rhoda Redler and Teresa Fall.*

Second Row-*Philip Chinnock, Gareth Pugh, Christopher Scaplehorn, David Waffington, Reine Riley, Christine Harris and Jean Charlton.*

First Row-*Adrena Miller, Hazel Leech, Freda Williams, Clive Palmer, Gaynor Tingle, Dorian Page, Lyndon Bengough and Graham Jones. (Absent that day were Anne Edwards, Vanessa Holt and Nic Velousan).*

The school years were not the happiest for Gareth.

"I had a bad stammer and on occasions the history teacher would ask me to read paragraphs from a book which I didn't like doing at all.

"Also, because I was of a small stature I was a target for bullies.

"Not good memories."

Gareth also remembers the time he was caned for smoking even though a cigarette had never touched his lips.

The cane was applied to the students' buttocks, calves, or palms of their hands in front of the class.

Sit-ups with ears pulled and arms crossed, kneeling, and standing on the bench in the classroom are other forms of punishment used in schools.

"I was giving four of the best, and I wasn't even smoking; I just happened to be with some boys who were.

"I tried to explain it to the headmaster, but he had none of it.

"When he opened the cane cupboard and asked which cane I wanted him to use, I said, 'none of them'.

"I then asked for the thickest cane to be used, but he wasn't buying it.

"He used a thin cane, which hurt much more than the thick one.

"Looking back, I should have had a school leaving certificate for mitching (playing truant).".

Gareth recalled that during one winter, the ground was frozen, so the pupils made an ice slide in the school's top yard.

"When it was my turn on the slide, I went down so fast that I went headfirst into a railing. I had such a wallop on the head that I didn't know where I was; my memory had gone. I was going from class to class, not knowing what was happening.

Eventually the teacher in the English class sensed something was wrong with me, and my older brother Gwyn was sent for, and I did not know him.

The headmaster took me home to Thurston Road, and because we never locked the front door, he took me into the house, sat me down, and left, so there I was, sitting on my own, not knowing what day of the week it was waiting for my parents to come home."

Then there was the time that Gareth's father took him up to Darran Mountain.

"When we managed to get up there, I had a perfect view of where we lived.

"Looking down, I told my father that I could see that our house had the worst roof in the street.

"He must have agreed because my uncle, Arthur Masters, put a new roof on the house.

"Of course, while the roof was being done, I had to have a look to see what was going on.

"There was no scaffolding, so I had to climb up a ladder."

Gareth was also part of the school's gymnastics team, which was another subject he really enjoyed.

"I was slight, so I could perform Barani flik flaks without a problem, and when it came to the gymnastics pyramid, of course I was always the top man."

A barani flik flak is a common move for gymnasts with a front flip combined with a half twist.

When done properly, a barani can be an impressive feat.

When not attending school, Gareth liked nothing more than going bird-nesting and stealing birds' eggs.

"I used to climb trees or even hang down quarries holding a clothes line.

"I can't believe that I used to risk my life doing that.

"Back then, all of us boys went bird-nesting.

"I suppose we knew it was wrong, but it was a learning curve for us.".

Gareth said, "When me and other boys used to go up the woods in Graig yr Esg, we would climb all over the rocks.

"There was an overhang right at the top that you couldn't get down to, so I decided to climb up to it.

"I got to a certain part when I realised my feet were not touching the rock face.

"I was simply climbing up with my hands only.

"I finally got to what I believed was a rooster's nest, which was empty and also really huge.

"It was so huge that I actually sat in it."

Ravens usually build their nests well above the ground, safe from predators and people.

Some pairs build a new nest each year, sometimes far away, although many will re-use their nests over several years, making repairs where necessary.

It was while sitting in the nest there that Gareth knew he faced a huge problem.

"I had to somehow get down."

"My pals could see me struggling and were telling me where to put my feet.

"Suddenly one of them shouted, 'We'll call the fire brigade.'

In a panic-stricken voice, Gareth shouted back, "No, don't do that!"

"My father works for the fire service, and he is on duty.

"If he was called out to this, I know I would be in for the hiding of my life.

"That was not going to happen."

Gareth said he was struggling so much to come down that he was near tears.

Somehow, Gareth managed to get his feet on solid ground.

"It was a huge relief, and after that, I never wanted to go back there again. It was very frightening."

Gareth can also recall one Christmas when his dad, who was a fireman based in Merthyr Fire Station, with the help of some of his fireman pals, made a wooden fort.

"It was a Christmas present, and my father tried to hide it, but me and my brother found it behind the couch."

After the school day was over, Gareth used to go to Rabaiotti's cafe in Pontypridd, where he would peel potatoes.

"I used to put the potatoes into something similar to a small cement mixer before peeling them, putting them in a chipping machine, and taking them up to the restaurant.

"The room where I was peeling potatoes had bottles of Blue Nun wine, and I used to knock on the tops of the bottles and guzzle the wine.

"The problem was that I needed to make sure I found and hid all the bottle tops, or I would be caught and there would be hell to pay.

"In another room, I also used to stock shelves.

"I was amazed at how many tobacco products were in there.

"There were all brands of cigarettes, cigars, pipe tobacco, and just about everything under the sun."

Gareth was always on the lookout to make a few bobs, and one opportunity came on Christmas time when he came across a tree full of holly.

He said, "I quickly cut the holly tree down and ran off."

While passing a nearby pub, Gareth shouted, "holly for sale," and the manager came out and bought the whole tree.

Meanwhile, on Thurston Road, there was a shop next door to the Pugh family home.

Gareth said, "The woman sadly died, so my mother took over the shop, which became our house.

"There were a lot of houses that had shops in them back in those days."

There was one morning at Pontsionorton School that Gareth will never forget.

He said, "The woodworking class was in Pontsionorton, and I was out in the yard when I could see all these vehicles going hell for leather along Merthyr Road.

"There were sirens going off, and goodness knows what.

"I then discovered that I had the afternoon off along with all the other schools in Pontypridd, which at the time I thought was brilliant.".

However, Gareth didn't know that the date was October 21, 1966, the day of the Aberfan disaster.

The Aberfan disaster was the catastrophic collapse of a colliery spoil tip.

Gareth's dad Arthur pictured in the middle at the top of picture was at the Aberfan disaster

The tip had been created on a mountain slope above the village of Aberfan and overlaid with a natural spring.

Heavy rain led to a buildup of water within the tip, which caused it to suddenly slide downhill as a slurry, killing 116 children and 28 adults as it engulfed Pantglas Junior School and a row of houses.

The tip was the responsibility of the National Coal Board (NCB), and the subsequent inquiry placed the blame for the disaster on the organisation.

"My father was based at Merthyr Fire Station, so he was one of the first to arrive at the scene of the disaster.

"He came home three days later, and he was physically and mentally drained over what he had witnessed."

With his school days now over, Gareth sets his sights on a working life.

2. Woodworking and the YMCA.

When Gareth was in Coedylan School every Tuesday morning, he used to travel to Pontsionorton School for a woodwork class.

The woodwork class was in a tin shed in the school yard. "In the tin shed was a Tortoise stove, which the teacher used to light.".

The Tortoise stove dates from 1830, when the first was hand-built by Charles Portway.

It was used to heat his ironmongery store in Halstead, Essex.

After making a second stove for a neighbour, Mrs. Portway suggested her husband go into business manufacturing and selling them. So he decided to establish a small foundry and went to work.

This proved so successful that in the next 50 years, over 17,000 of his stoves were sold, providing low-cost and economical heating for many thousands of people.

Gareth said, "We would put a pot of glue on the stove that was suspended in a can of water to always keep it warm.

"I'll never forget the smell of that glue.

"It is what I would call a memory smell—something you will never forget.

"The woodwork teacher was Mr. Mower, who was a wonderful teacher; he was truly amazing.

"He taught the class first to make a bench hook, and what astonished me most was that while he was showing us how to make one, he had his thumb right up against the saw blade.

"It looked dangerous to me, but I soon found out that he was guiding the blade."

Gareth said the first thing he ever made in the woodwork class was a letter rack, which he said was "a bit crummy."

"The second thing I made was a bit more adventurous.

"It was a square stool interwoven with raffia or something like that on the top.

"I think that back then every schoolboy who attended the carpentry class made those stools because a lot of houses had one."

Gareth recalled that back in his school woodworking days, he had to pay for the wood he used to make items.

"Wood was quite expensive back then.

"I wanted to make a wardrobe, which was a bit ambitious.

"Anyway, I did make one out of good-quality plywood and timber, and it cost my mother ten shillings (50 pence) for the wood.

"That was a considerable amount back then.

"While I was making the wardrobe, I had to take a shilling (5p) into class each week to cover the cost.

"After I finished the wardrobe, it was shown, along with other woodworking items, at an exhibition to let people know what sort of things we were making."

During his woodworking years, Gareth said that twice a year he would use a lathe to turn matchstick barrels.

"I can also remember getting the wood ready to make a bowl using only a hand saw to cut every corner off until it was almost round.

"But of course nowadays, a band saw would be used to do it."

Woodworking was without doubt Gareth's favourite school subject and also the one in which he never failed to come top of the class.

And of course, every three weeks, the class used to have technical drawings.

A technical drawing is a detailed, precise diagram or plan to show how an item is constructed.

"I was rubbish at math, but I got to grips with the technical drawing, and lo and behold, on numerous occasions, I came at the at the top of the class in that as well.

"I did really well in the woodwork class, and I put it down to the teacher, Mr. Mower.

"He was a great help to me."

Gareth's woodworking skill proved to be a benefit to him in his working life.

"When I started roofing, I could cut rafters, fascias, and soffits, but I wanted more than that, so I decided to build a shed so I could have a lathe, which was something I always wanted.

"So, I purchased the biggest one I could get and also one I could afford.".

Gareth also became a member of the YMCA in Pontypridd. He said, "They used to have a table tennis room there, which was good.

"You used to have to put your name on a board to book a game.

"If you were a good player, you would keep playing on the table until someone beats you.

"I enjoyed playing table tennis. I could hold my own. I was light on my feet, which was a bonus.

Gareth recalled that there was one time there was this tall lad in the table tennis room who he had seen earlier in Ynysyngharad Park.

"I think I must have said something to him that he didn't like, but I didn't think any more of it.

"Anyway, I was playing table tennis with a friend when a girl came in the room and said that there was a basketball game going on in the top hall.

"The tall lad who I had met earlier had seen me and said that he was going to get me and my mate.

"Well, I was having none of that, so I said to my pal, 'let's not wait for him. He's playing basketball, so let's go and get him now.'

"So, the next thing that happened was the two of us burst into the basketball game and jumped on the tall lad.

"Of course, when they realised what was going on, both teams turned on us and started to give us a hiding.

"We couldn't get out of there fast enough and ran down the stairs, taking some punches, before fleeing down Taff Street.

"I had my shirt ripped off my back and was shedding some blood.

"While we were making our escape, I shouted to my pal that I would see him on Saturday night at a dance they were holding in the YMCA's Shelley Hall.

The historic and iconic Shelley Hall has been an integral part of the Pontypridd YMCA since its initial opening in 1910.

"Come Saturday, some of the basketball players were there waiting for us.

"I sensed there was trouble ahead.

"They started poking me and asking where my friends were.

"Little did they know that we were quietly entering the hall in pairs.

"I was chosen to start the fight, so I went up to the tall guy, and I hit him.

"The next thing that happened was that I was seeing stars when a boy grabbed me by the throat and another one was going to squash me into the wall.

"But I will never forget this lad named Steffan coming to my rescue when he side swiped one of them.

"He saved me from getting a proper hiding before everything started to calm down.

"The strange thing was that when all the fighting was over, everybody became pals.

"It was all friendly, with everyone respecting each other.

"That's the way it was back then."

Gareth also recalled the dances being held in Pontypridd's Municipal Hall.

Originally a Wesleyan chapel and built in 1895 by Arthur O Evans, architect of Pontypridd, adopting the then fashionable scheme of combining chapel and Sunday school in a unified composition.

It later became a Municipal Hall.

It was converted in the 1980s to an arts centre with a theatre, gallery and café.

"Mind you if any trouble started there it was soon sorted out by the bouncers who were big blokes.

"There was no messing about back then".

3. Mitching School and Bird Nesting

GARETH didn't like school and said he would often go mitching (playing truancy) from school.

Gareth remembers one time, when he was mitching, that he went to the baths in Ynysyngharad Park (pictured).

"The baths were one of the favourite places for boys to go mitching.

"There was one time, however, when the Whipper In (school truancy officer) called into the baths when me and other boys were there.

"He could see us by the side of the water while we spotted him in the cafe window, so we dived in and were bobbing around the fountains they had there.

"He couldn't get near us, and eventually he just gave up."

Gareth has great memories of his visits to the baths.

"Me and a lot of other boys practically lived down there.

"It was a three-pence entry fee, but when we didn't have any three-penny bits, we would just go over the wall.".

During his many visits to the baths, Gareth got friendly with the lifeguards and staff members.

"One day this chap came in, and we all thought he looked like somebody special.

"Suddenly, he put his hand in his pocket and pulled out a lot of silver coins and threw them in the deep end of the pool.

"Of course, we all dived in, and I remember fighting underwater with a lifeguard to get at the silver coins, and I managed to get more than my fair share of them.

"We used to practice diving into the pool to pull up a box full of lead, which was a sort of training exercise for us."

He said, "I know mitching was wrong, but the school years were a very difficult time for me.

"I had a stammer, which at times was embarrassing, particularly when I had to read something in class.

"But that wasn't all.

"I was often the target of bullies, but having said that, I used to give as good as I got.

"I was on the school's gymnastics team, while I also enjoyed the woodwork and technical drawing."

When not in school, Gareth began to take an interest in bird nesting.

"It was a craze back then for myself and other boys to collect birds' eggs, although when I look back at it now, I realise how dreadful it was.

"But it was a different time back then; for instance, everybody smoked cigarettes, which is considered a very bad habit nowadays."

BBC 4's Natural History program stated on their web site that "the bird nesting hobby was not restricted to children and that egg collectors would swap or trade with one another, and competition became fevered among wealthy or intrepid collectors.

"Enthusiasts vied with each other to go to more and more extreme lengths to collect the eggs.

"One famous collector named Charles Bendire was willing to have his teeth broken to remove an egg that had become stuck in his mouth after he had placed it there for safekeeping after climbing down a tree.".

The first nest Gareth found was a rare grasshopper warbler's nest under a bank near a river in Eglwysilan.

The Grasshopper Warbler is found scattered across the UK in summer, although it is less common in Scotland.

It likes areas of scrub, thick grassland, the edges of reedbeds, new forestry plantations, and gravel pits with plenty of scattered bushes.

Gareth also discovered there was a publication called *The Observer Book of Birds Eggs*.

The *Observer's Book of Bird's Eggs* is part of a series of small, pocket-sized books, published by Frederick Warne and Co in the United Kingdom from 1937 to 2003.

The books covered a range of topics such as hobbies, art, history and wildlife.

The aim of the books was to interest children.

Some of them have become collector's items.

"That book, cost five shillings(25p) but it was brilliant.

"It was like our bible."

Gareth also recalled the time he again mitched school and went bird nesting in Eglwysilan.

"One of the birds' eggs I never had was from a curlew.

"I could see them flying around up there but I could never figure out where they were flying to."

The curlew's nest is a shallow cup formed in the grass sward by swiveling and pressing down to flatten the grass.

The curlew usually lays up to four eggs, but fewer eggs may be laid, particularly if birds are older or the nest is a second attempt to replace an earlier loss.

The nests are usually difficult to find.

Gareth said, "So I used to go up to Eglwysilan and bury myself in the heather, stay perfectly still, and watch where the curlews landed.

"But they used to outsmart me because when they landed, it wasn't anywhere near their nests, so in all my years of bird nesting, I never found a curlew's nest."

For young Gareth, following his passion for bird nesting didn't come without any risks.

"I had some close escapes.

"I heard on the grapevine that a sparrowhawk's nest had been found up on the Pontypridd Golf Links in a squirrel's drey.".

Sparrowhawks build their nests in trees in forests and woodlands virtually throughout the UK. The nest is usually built low in a tree, in a fork near an opening where they have easy access. Sparrowhawk nests are built from twigs and not lined with soft material. They can reach nearly a meter wide and about 30 centimetres deep, although most are smaller.

"So, when I heard about the sparrowhawk's nest, I had to go and find out.

"Anyway, I climbed a tall silver birch tree just about to the top, and when I shoved my hand in the drey, a squirrel jumped out and ran over my face and down my back.

"How I didn't fall off that tree, I will never know."

After collecting birds' eggs, what did Gareth decide to do with them?

"I couldn't keep the eggs in my house because my father didn't approve of it, so I used to keep them in a house belonging to a close friend of mine called Keith Harris.

"Keith used to keep them in a drawer in the front room, which he lined with cotton wool.

"After blowing the contents of the eggs out, we would sometimes varnish them before labelling them.".

Gareth said that some of the eggs that were stored away were quite rare.

"Anyway, Keith left the drawer open one day, and his cat walked all over them, and that signaled the end of my bird nesting days.

"But when I look back at those bird nests, I have good and bad thoughts about them.

"I often think how wrong it was, but on the other hand, the benefits were learning about nature.

"We discovered what nests looked like and what time of the year the birds flew back.

"It was a case of learning a lot about ornithology.

"It really pleases me now to see a kingfisher darting up the river or watch the swifts flying."

4. Being an ATC cadet and Pop bottle refunds.

GARETH also recalled the time in the 1960s when he was a cadet at the ATC (Air Training Corps) in Treforest.

"I really enjoyed being part of the ATC.

"I have great memories of attending there.

"It was one shilling (5p) a week and there were activities like abseiling, canoeing, gliding, flying and shooting 303 rifles".

One of the Air Training Corps unique activities is flying when cadets of all ages are able to experience powered flight.

They are also able to perform their own aerobatic techniques under the instruction of Ex or Current RAF pilots.

These are called Air Experience Flights or AEF for short.

Gareth remembers on one aerobatics occasion in St Athans he was sat with a pilot in a Chipmunk aeroplane.

The de Havilland Canada DHC-1 Chipmunk is a tandem, two-seat, single-engine primary trainer aircraft designed and developed by Canadian aircraft manufacturer de Havilland Canada.

It was developed shortly after the Second World War and sold in large numbers during the immediate post-war years.

"The pilot asked how many flying hours I had done, and I told him I had completed ten, but I bent the truth a bit because I had only completed one.

"Because he believed I had completed ten he let me take control of the plane.

"It was brilliant.

"I eased the joystick back and did a loop.

"I loved it.

"While I was there, I also recall learning how to shoot a 303 Enfield rifle.

"I was only 13 years old, and I used to lay down on a ground sheet and fire at a target, which was, I think, about 300 yards away.

"I'll never forget the recoil of the rifle when I fired it.

"It nearly pushed me off the ground sheet.".

With his school days over in 1968, Gareth soon started work.

"My first job was with a local company called Jones Brothers.

"I was a tea boy on a building site in Graigwen.

"I think back then the band of new semi-detached houses being built there cost about £3,500."

"My wage was £5 a week, so I would give my mother £3, and I would keep the rest.

"Besides my job, I was always doing bits and bobs, and if I never had enough money for something I needed, my mother would always help me out.

"I used to make tea for the workers during their breaks, and every dinner time I used to be given a list and a wheelbarrow and told to go to a nearby shop at the top of Graigwen to get pop and food for the workers.

"Often, I had to take empty Corona pop bottles back, and in those days, you would get deposit money back when you returned them. I think it was about three pennies off a bottle.".

The glass bottles in which Corona Pop was sold were a valuable commodity, and the Porth-based Thomas and Evans company operated a system of money back on the bottle.

This ensured that generations of schoolchildren would augment their pocket money by collecting discarded bottles.

Gareth said, "I suppose, when you think about it now, taking empty bottles back in those days was a form of recycling.

"Of course, when I got back from my wheelbarrow shopping trip, the workers would ask for the refunded 'pop bottle money,' but there was no way they were going to get it.

"The only place the empty bottle money was going, was in my pocket."

Gareth soon had his fill of being a building site tea boy, so he packed it in.

He then got a job as a van boy with Pontypridd-based Mother's Pride Bakery, which was on East Street in Trallwn, Pontypridd.

He said, "In the 1960s, you could walk out of one job and walk straight back into another.

"That's the way it was back then.

"There is a lot of history about the bakery, which goes back to a chap called Hopkin Morgan.".

Hopkin Morgan

Hopkin Morgan was born in Llantwit Fardre in 1854 and when he left school at the age of 14, he set up a small bakery in his home.

He used to carry loaves around in a basket which were quickly bought by local people. Hopkin Morgan increased his loaf selling business so much that he needed a horse and cart which was then replaced by vehicles.

Hopkin Morgan, later became Mother's Pride Bakery.

Gareth said: "At one time the bakery had its own branch line on the Glamorganshire Canal to get flour into the bakery."

The Glamorganshire Canal in South Wales, UK, was begun in 1790.

It ran along the valley of the River Taff from Merthyr Tydfil to the sea at Cardiff.

The final section of the canal was closed in 1951.

Gareth used to start work at 6am in the bakery before going out on his rounds.

He said: "My van driver back then was Glyn Henshaw, who I believe was from Porth.

"Our first stop was the Dunlop Semtex Rubber factory in Brynmawr".

Dunlop Semtex achieved success with the factory, producing flooring for the health and education sectors, before going on to buy the site in 1964.

A downturn in fortunes in the late 1970s and early 1980s led to the factory's closure in 1981.

"We used to deliver bread there for vending machines and the women there were quite mischievous always doing practical jokes.

"You never knew what they would get up to

"I can well remember one occasion in particular when a workman was walking around with a raw sausage hanging from his fly.

"I tried every way to get his attention but when I turned around the women were laughing their heads off behind my back because they had set me up.

"I was 16 at the time and I was so embarrassed I didn't know where to look.

"Mind you I had my own back when I was locked in a fridge with a woman which ended up with her running out screaming.

"We had a great laugh about it afterwards.

"Our bread rounds then were in Brynmawr, Gilwern and Crickhowell.

"Twice a week we would deliver bread to the Cwrt-y-Gollen army camp in Crickhowell".

Cwrt-y-Gollen became the regional centre for infantry training as the Welsh Brigade Depot in 1963.

"Christmas time was particularly busy because of the demand for fresh bread we had to make two deliveries so that meant an early start.

"We would always try to arrive there at lunchtime so we could have a bite to eat.

"Anyway, while we were there one day a staff sergeant was frying eggs on a hot plate.

"He had two eggs in his hand which he cracked and put them on the hot plate just using his one hand.

"He turned to me and said: 'I bet you can't to that'.

"Well, he turned out to be wrong because I did do it but having said that it was pure luck and was something I could never do again."

Gareth can also recall a time when a show of his hands ended up in a court case.

"I don't know how it happened but one day I was on the Newport round and of course while out delivering we were handling jam doughnuts and bread which were on runners on the aluminium shelves.

"Because of this our hands used to get black.

"Now and again, we used to ask shop owners if we could wash our hands, and they were always very obliging.

"Anyway, one day a Public Health Inspector came on the van and asked to see our hands".

A Public Health Inspector is responsible for carrying out measures for protecting public health and providing support to minimize health and safety hazards.

"When the Inspector saw how black our hands were he was disgusted and of course we were reported.

"What happened next was I had to make several visits to a solicitor in Newport and the outcome was a court case brought by the Public Health Inspector against Mothers Pride.

"It was a really big case with the Mother's Pride top brass and the Press in attendance.

"If it was proved that we were in the wrong then all wholesale delivery vans would need to be fitted with wash basins which would result in a staggering expense.

"On the day of the court case I was called to the witness box and a barrister asked me how far away the Inspector was when he looked at my hands.

"I told him I wasn't very good with distances so I couldn't really say.

"Then he asked me to point out to someone in the courtroom to gauge what I thought the distance would have been.

"So, guess who I pointed to?

"The Health and Safety Inspector.

"Of all the people in the courtroom I had to point at him.

"People in the courtroom couldn't get over it. There was uproar there."

"At the end of the case no action was taken against Mother's Pride.

"We got away with it.

"Not long after that I had to pack the job in.

They were paying me £17 a week, which I suppose was too much and I was getting too old to be a van boy.

"I have fond memories of working for Mother's Pride especially meeting many people which was part of the job I really liked."

5. When Steptoe called into the Rose and Crown.

Gareth's mother Lilian pictured with Harry H Corbett and Linda Thorson.

GARETH also has wonderful memories of the time in the 1970s when his mother and stepdad Don ran the Rose and Crown pub in Eglwysilan.

The Rose and Crown pub, which closed in 2021, is well-known for its unique location and beautiful views over the Taff and Aber valleys.

Located next to St Llan's church on the mountainside above Abertridwr the popular pub was also featured on the Sky Tv's *Stella*, created by *Gavin and Stacey* creator Ruth Jones.

"They were special years," recalled Gareth, "the pub was never short of customers and there was always some sort of entertainment going on."

One lasting memory is when actor Harry H Corbett the star of *Steptoe and Son* and Linda Thorson visited the pub to collect a £2,000 cheque for the Muscular Dystrophy charity.

Harry H. Corbett OBE, who died in 1982, was an English actor and comedian, best remembered for playing rag-and-bone man Harold Steptoe alongside Wilfrid Brambell in the long-running BBC television sitcom Steptoe and Son.

Linda Thorson, pictured with Harry H Corbett and Gareth's mother Lilian, is a Canadian actress, known for playing Tara King on *The Avengers*.

Gareth said: "My wonderful mother loved nothing more than raising money for good causes".

Gareth said that they would sometimes have a folk group performing in the pub which was always packed.

"My mother and the staff were really busy behind the bar and were struggling to cope so she asked me to go on the door to stop people coming in.

"Anyway, people would come to the door expecting to go in, but I used to apologise and say that the place was full.

"There was no room at the pub.

"But then I would say that if they bought me a pint of beer, I would turn a blind eye and let them in.

"So, in no time at all I had a windowsill full of pints, so I soon got well and truly smashed.

"Of course when my mother found out and that was it. I never went on the door again."

Gareth started his roofing career with Peter Thomas who had a business on Pentrebach Road in Pontypridd.

He said: "It was a new line of work for me, and I was a complete novice but having said that everybody helped each other out".

Gareth said there were ups and downs while working there and he was sacked seven times.

"One of the sacking times came about after we were doing a job in Porthcawl where I was a foreman on what was called the Forty Acre Site.

"Anyway, a driver came down to the job we were working on with an articulated lorry full of tiles.

"The lorry's trailer was parked on the main road so we made a ramp out of trestles and planks to go over the garden and on to the ladder to go up and over the roof. Of course there was no scaffolding back then.

"There were four of us on the site and we hadn't taken long to load up the tiles and take them over to the back of the roof.

"The driver then asked me to give him a hand to take the tiles off the ramp and stack them on the ground".

But there was no way that Gareth was going to let that happen.

"I told him that it would only take about 20 minutes to carry the tiles up on to the front of the roof because it would be easier than carrying them to the back.

"I didn't want to have an argument about it because after all we were both working for the same company.

"Because I had refused and told the other roofers not to do it when I got back to the yard, I was given the sack but I wasn't sacked for long because I always got a phone call to go back.

"While I was roofing with Peter Thomas one of the workers used to take his dog to work.

"His dog used to run up the pole ladder and would be on the roof with us all day long.

"But at the end of the shift we had to put him on our shoulders to take him down cos he couldn't get back down the ladder."

There were two jobs in Weymouth that Gareth will always remember.

"For the job we had a land rover with a lorry back attached to it and a trailer.

"There were three of us and we had all the materials for a re-roofing job.

"We were loaded with 500 tiles, sand, cement, felt, battens the lot.

"So we set off heading for Newport to get on the M4 motorway and while we were driving along a lorry behind kept flashing us.

"We pulled over and discovered we had lost a wheel off the trailer which incredibly we never realised had happened.

"We had all this gear in the trailer, and we just didn't know what to do.

"I managed to get to a phone and rang my uncle Arthur Masters who worked as a driver for Peter Thomas, and he came along with an articulated lorry, and we piled everything on that.

"So, the two boys went in the land rover, and I joined my uncle in the artic and we did eventually get the job done."

The other job Gareth did in Weymouth was at the Alexandra hotel which was right on the seafront.

Gareth said: "We were staying in the hotel which had a parapet wall on the front, so we didn't need scaffolding and we used to climb out of the dormer windows in our bedrooms and then climb on to the hotel's roof.

"I had relatives in Weymouth, and I remember one night the roofers decided to enjoy themselves at a night club, but I didn't go because I had arranged to meet my relatives in a pub in the town.

"The weather was really bad.

"The heavens opened. We had the roof covered with felt and battens.

The Alexandra hotel

"Anyway, when I got back to the hotel the hotel manager told me there was water coming through the roof.

"Some of the felt had blown back so I knew I had to get on the roof.

"I looked out of the window and could see it was still hammering down.

"Don't ask me why, but I decided to strip down to my underpants.

"It must have been around midnight when I decided to climb up on to the roof in my underpants to put the felt right.

"Suddenly the night was lit up with blue flashing lights.

"An elderly lady had called the police to report a burglar on the roof of the hotel.

"The police must have thought the burglar on the roof was a pervert trying to break in wearing only his underpants.

"When I did come down everyone was cracking up with laughter."

Gareth has also recollections of the roofing times when he had "close calls."

"Working on roofs back then meant climbing a ladder and carrying supplies on our shoulders.

"That was the case while I was working for Peter Thomas on a site in Boverton when I was carrying a pack of four six metre lengths of plastic verge units up the ladder in a gale force wind.

"I had reached the top of the roof when a blast of wind turned the units into what I can only describe as an aircraft wing, which blew me backwards making me let go of the units which resulted in me landing on the bottom course of tiles.

"Meanwhile the units went sailing down and were smashed into smithereens.

"When we packed up for the day and went back to the yard in Pontypridd there was carnage.

"There were whole roofs blown off because of the gale force wind.

"We were inundated with calls from people wanting their damaged roofs repaired".

Another close call Gareth will never forget happened again while Working for Peter Thomas on the roof of a clothes shop in Porthcawl town centre.

He said: "The back of the building was three storeys high and once again it was no scaffolding just ladders.

"I had a bucket of cement in front of me while working with a trowel on an abutment wall.

"The bucket slipped knocking my feet from under me and I slid down the roof tiles and my toes ended up getting caught in the gutter.

"All this was happening when I was on the third storey of the building with spiked railings directly underneath me.

"Somehow I managed to scramble back up, finish the job and got the hell out of there."

Then there was the time that Gareth was working on a site in Llantwit Major, along with three other roofers, and they each shared around 3,500 tiles to carry on their shoulders while climbing a ladder.

"We were in a relay going up the ladder and sometimes we would have to wait for each other to climb the ladder which slowed everything down.

"A big pile of sand had been tipped, which was needed for the job, so I decided to run off the roof and do a long jump into the sand and grab a bundle of tiles before climbing back up the ladder.

"And of course in those days we used to have a bit of fun and race against each other while our own rows of tiles were on the roof.

"So, the others started copying me and the race was on".

Suddenly a chap approached Gareth and said: "What do you lot think you lot are doing?".

Gareth just looked at him and said: "What's it got to do with you.?"

The chap then said: "I'll tell you what it has got to do with me. I'm the safety officer and I want you lot off the site now."

So, Gareth and the other roofers had to pack up and leave the site.

Gareth said: "What I found incredible about it was that this man, the safety officer, had us thrown off the site for something very minor yet we were putting ourselves at risk working on ladders without any scaffolding which I thought was unbelievable."

While working for Peter Thomas Gareth found himself doing a roofing job on his own in Aberdare.

He said: "I had a pair of roofs to do myself, which I knew I would get extra money for, so I travelled up there on my Java CZ 175 motor bike.

"The two roofs had already been battened so I just needed to tile it up and tidy the job up.

"I got there about 7.30am and I carried 180 bundles of seven tiles up onto the roof.

"How I did it I don't know but I had finished the roof and after jumping on my Java I was back home in Ponty by four o'clock and best of all I had £35 for doing the job.

"It was a real bonus for me for at the time I was earning £45 a week.

"When we used to do an up and over back then a terraced house was costing about £180.

"The funny thing was in those days that's all the householders were concerned about was the colour of the tiles which were concrete, interlocking and granite finish.

"Strange but true.

"We soon discover that the roofs were not constructed to take the weight of the tiles."

After about seven years Gareth packed his job in with Peter Thomas.

In 1976 Rhondda born actor Stanley Baker was given a knighthood while the Wales rugby team won the Grand Slam in the Five Nations championship. On the music front Swansea born singer Bonnie Tyler had a hit with a song called *Lost in France* and Gareth was now working for Treforest Roofing with a bloke called Mike Marley.

It was the same year that Gareth's 18-year-old younger brother Berwyn got killed while riding a motor bike on Llantrisant Road, Tonteg.

Berwyn is pictured with family pet Rex.

A Talbot Queen inquest was told that Berwyn was riding his motorcycle in Llantwit Road, Tonteg, when he collided with a car which was being driven in the opposite direction.

The car driver and his wife were trapped inside the vehicle because the release buttons were engulfed in flames.

Giving evidence PC John Morgan said the motorcycle's petrol tank was made of fibre glass.

Following the collision the fibre glass had cracked or exploded on impact result in pouring petrol in through the shattered car.

Following the inquest on Berwyn coroner Owen Rees said that Berwyn's parents, especially his father Arthur (pictured) who was at the scene, suffered greatly along with the occupants of the car.

A verdict of accidental death was returned.

It was a time when Gareth's father Arthur was in the Fire Service.

He attended the call out but was busy dealing with the burning car involved in the accident, not realising his son was lying on the road with a nurse who was trying to resuscitate him.

Gareth said: "My father didn't know until he got back to the fire station. It was an awful time for the family.

"Back then I owned a Triumph Bonneville motor bike but after what happened to Berwyn I got rid of it.

"I bought a reliant three-wheeler car which I called *The Dalek*."

So, Gareth eventually decided to pack his job in with Treforest Roofing and applied for a job in the Ford Factory in Bridgend.

The Ford Bridgend Engine Plant was an internal combustion engine factory owned by Ford of Europe. Between 1980 and 2020, it made over 22 million engines used in Ford, Volvo, Jaguar and Land Rover cars. Ford closed the Bridgend plant on 25 September 2020.

Gareth said: "I had passed the interview and then I had to travel to Bridgend to have a medical test.

"When I arrived, I urgently needed to have a pee, so I found a toilet and relieved myself.

"When I was called in for the test, I was asked to give a urine sample and of course that was a major problem because I had just used the toilet.

"But anyway, I managed to do it and I thankfully I was offered a job."

Before Gareth go start his new job he was contacted by local roofer Mel Bolderson.

"Mel asked me if I would like to work for him but I told him I had got the job with the Ford company with a really good wage of £75 a week along with a pension and what have you.

"But Mel wouldn't be put off and said he would match the wage and the pension and petrol money and other things.

"Looking back, I did my best to get the best deal out of him and it worked so I took up his job offer."

There was another close call for Gareth while he was working for roofer Mel Bolderson.

He said: "I was working on the spire at St Catherine's Church in Upper Church Street, Pontypridd.

"The spire is 162 feet high, and I was hauling a pulley and pulling up a bundle of two metres long battens.

"Anyway, the middle batten slipped out of the bundle as I was pulling it up.

"There were also stone masons working on the spire and they had a water tank which was being used to pump up water to wash the stonework.

"A stone mason who was standing by the water tank happened to turn his head when the batten which was like downward missile went through the tank water and embedded itself about a foot into the ground and didn't even make a splash.

"If the stone mason had not turned his head while the batten was plummeting, I dread to think what might have happened."

Gareth said he was working with Mel Phillips doing lead work on top of the spire and also restoring the weathervane.

"We took the scrap lead off the top and instead of carrying it down from that height I decided to just drop it down.

"I had a walkie talkie, and I made sure that workers underneath would be well away while I was dropping the lead down.

"At that time there were big fir trees at the front of St Catherine's.

"I had hold of a lump of lead, weighing around two or three pounds, which I hurled out into the air, and which landed right where I wanted it to land on the church path.

"Then I got hold of another piece of lead which was a lot heavier.

"And so, I decided to put more muscle power into throwing it.

"Before I knew it the lump of lead went sailing through the air towards the busy traffic travelling up and down the main road near the church.

"But by the grace of God it shot through the fir trees and landed in the ground about two or three feet from the edge of the roadway".

One Saturday Gareth was working on his own at St Catherine's when the church bells rang out during a wedding ceremony.

"I was working on the steeple and the bells sounded I had placed a rule against the steeple which moved four inches which was the sign of a good structure".

"Anyway, when we had finished St Catherine's spire the scaffolders were dropping the scaffold and we noticed that the band of lead going round you know the top part, the top six metres, had lifted.

"Now this bit of lead was around six pounds per square foot so it's very thick lead.

"So, we stopped the scaffolders, and we put a wooden pole ladder on the scaffolding to go up and push it back down with a lead dresser.

"Anyway, our wooden pole ladder wouldn't reach so in our wisdom we tied another on to that.

"So, I went up there and I had three or four of them holding the bottom of the ladder on top of the scaffold and I went up with the lead dresser in my pocket but as I went up the top ladder slewed to the side so I was hanging out.

"So, it was decided that I get back down a bit sharpish while the scaffolders raised the scaffold up so that we could reach that piece of lead.

"I honestly think that they must have moved the lead off the scaffold pole or plank or something.

"It was quite a close call.

"It was something that could have happened in an old comedy film starring Buster Keaton.

On another occasion while working in the Baptist Chapel in Trallwn that Gareth "saw the light."

"One of the chapel people came over to the yard and asked if any of us could put a light bulb on the cross on the gable end at the top of the chapel.

"I said of course I would have a go, but the problem was I didn't have a ladder that long.

"No problem" he said "I've got one."

Gareth said the ladder had a triple extension and described it as "massive."

"Anyway, to get to the cross we had to go out into the middle of the road with the ladder which was on pulleys.

"Eventually we managed to get right underneath the cross and of course it just happened to be down to me to go up.

"So armed with the light bulb up I climbed up the wooden ladder.

"I had no trouble climbing up the first section.

"But when I got up to the top section it was so far up the top of the ladder was pressed tight against the wall and I was standing on the third rung from the top with nothing to hold on to.

"My knees were shaking but I managed to get the old bulb out and put the new one in before getting to terra firma pronto.

"It really was one of the scariest things I ever did."

Gareth worked for 18 years for Mel Bolderson and said: "Mel was firm but fair. I learned a lot while working for him."

GOOD HABIT

While working for Mel Bolderson Gareth was also a roadie (a person employed by a touring band of musicians to set up and maintain equipment) for a group that was called Good Habit.

Good Habit were a Welsh professional touring band, mostly from Penarth active from 1970 until 1975.

They had one single called *Find My Way Back Home*.

The band played at music festivals including the first Glastonbury Festival.

Good Habit later changed their name to Racing Cars.

Racing Cars was a Welsh pop band, formed in the Rhondda Valley in 1973.

Their only hit single was *They Shoot Horses, Don't They?*

The song peaked at number fourteen in the UK Singles Chart in 1977.

The song was inspired by the film, *They Shoot Horses, Don't They?*

During their tour the band included dates supporting rock group Bad Company.

Gareth Mortimer, who was also known as Morty, was the front man of the Rhondda based band.

Originally from Maerdy, Morty, (pictured) who sadly passed away in 2015 at the age of 66, was one of the most successful artists to come out of the Valleys.

Morty got together with guitarist, Graham Headley Williams, and along with Ray 'Alice' Ennis (guitar), David Land (bass) and Robert Wilding (drums) they formed Racing Cars.

Touring to promote their debut releases, Racing Cars backed Bad Company in 1976, including dates at Earls Court and the York Theatre Royal.

Eventually, the pressure of punk and new wave music, combined with increasing indifference from their record label led to the band splitting up in the early '80s.

But Morty remained a presence in the music business, releasing a solo album, touring America and singing back-up vocals with the Beach Boys, Tina Turner and Bryan Adams.

In 1981, Morty joined a band called The Bleeding Hearts with musicians Paul Rosser, Bob Watkins and Dave Iles, and Morty suggested they call themselves Racing Cars.

When this band came to an end, Morty, Graham Hedley Williams and Paul Rosser reunited and they continued to play gigs across Europe, launching a new album, *Bolt from the Blue*.

"I remember one gig when Good Habit were playing in Caldicot when myself and a couple of others set all the equipment up.

"After we finished, I went for a pint in the bar and while I was there one of the band members asked if I could work on the audio mixing machine which was a contraption raised upon the centre of the dance floor with a load of switches".

An audio mixer is an electronic device that allows you to combine and adjust different audio signals from various sources, such as microphones and instruments, to produce a better sound output.

"I told him that I had never done it before, and he said just fiddle around with a couple of the switches and look important.

"So I got up on to the stage and boy oh boy wasn't I the cat's whiskers.

The girls were dancing around me and it goes without me saying that I really enjoyed that".

Gareth recalls another time when the band was invited on a guest list with a rock band called Thin Lizzy in the Top Rank in Cardiff.

Thin Lizzy are an Irish hard rock band formed in Dublin in 1969.

In 1986 Phil Lynott, the former lead singer of Thin Lizzy, died from heart failure and pneumonia after an 11-day fight for his life.

Gareth said: "There was a huge queue to get into the Top Rank.

"But we passed them all and went straight in which was fabulous.

"The backing group there was named String Driven Thing and they were brilliant".

String Driven Thing are a Scottish folk-rock band, formed in Glasgow in 1967 and led by married couple Chris and Pauline Adams, with the electric violin of Graham Smith.

6. Roofing with a Lada Car.

WHILE working as a foreman for Mel Bolderson Gareth said as time went on the roofing business was slowly declining.

He said: "In the end the workforce went down to four three and eventually just me.

"Mel then offered me a job as a manager of a new yard on Treforest Trading estate or I could take redundancy.

Gareth working on a roof in Mountain Ash belonging to Andrew Bush of Bush and Griffiths Building Supplies.

"For the 18 years I was there I was offered £4,000, which I owed him half of that because I was always struggling to raise money to get a vehicle.

"I went to the Labour Exchange in Pontypridd and told a woman staff member that I wanted to start my own business and if there was any way that I could get some support in doing this.

"The woman was quite taken aback and told me that there was a course available on Treforest Trading Estate.

"I'll never forget the chap who was taking the course, his name was Eddie Spillane.

"I couldn't get over his name because what came into my head was Mickey Spillane who was an American gangster."

Gareth said the course concentrated more on the business side of things because the people who attended knew the practical side, they knew their jobs.

"I had plenty of support from that course. It was very beneficial."

Gareth received a business startup grant of £1,500 which was paid out in stages.

"It was ideal for me. It helped me buy a van because at the time I was doing my roofing work with a Lada car and I was somehow managing to get by.

"It was quite funny how I managed to acquire the Lada car.

"I got it by making a swap with a set of darts".

Gareth was on a roofing job in Creigiau when a chap took an interest in the Lada and offered to buy it for £450.

"I refused his offer and told him that I needed the car for my roofing work but if I did manage to buy a van, I would sell it to him for £500.

"Anyway, he came back a few days later and paid me the £500 and wasn't bothered about any documentation.

"He really wanted the Lada.

"Lada cars at the time were being shipped to Russia because they couldn't get the spare parts.

"They were being stripped down and any unwanted parts were thrown overboard."

Gareth was now self-employed and working on his own was his biggest challenge to get enough work.

"I was getting by because I was fortunate in getting work from some of Mel Bolderson's old customers.

"I was able to choose what customers I would work for because like a lot of businesses it was inevitable that you would get one or two customers who were slow making payments.

Gareth pictured working on a roof in Creigiau.

"There was one customer who offered me work on a couple of roofs, but I turned him down and when he wanted to know why I told him that I couldn't afford to do the work for him because he was too slow in making payments".

Gareth was now using scaffolding and became very friendly with a local scaffolder named Tony Griffiths.

"Tony and his workers were really good and did cracking jobs for me."

In the early 2000s Gareth remarried and his wife's name was Lorraine.

"Lorraine had family in Devon and I used to get work there including barn conversions (pictured) and the added bonus was that I was able to stay over there and do some fishing.

"They were lovely people and always gave me the best of welcomes."

With his work finished in the West Country Gareth found himself working on a building site in Ponthir near Newport.

He was working there on a site where a company were doing roofing work in London.

"Anyway, me and a young worker I had at the time were offered some work in London.

"I decided to take up the offer and so we ended up staying in a caravan next to the job which was just off the Old Kent Road.

"I found it very intimidating while working in London. I didn't like big city life."

Gareth said that close to the site was a pub called The Lord Nelson, whose customers were mostly Irish.

"I knew straight away that the pub was a bit like a cowboy saloon you would see in the movies cos there was a bit of damage there caused through fighting.

"Having said it was a great atmosphere in there and I always felt comfortable although the London Pride beer they served there was awful, so I stuck to bottles of Newcastle Brown".

Gareth recalled that one Saturday night, while most of the site worker had gone home for the weekend he sat in the pub.

He said: "It was near closing time, and I was just about to leave when the landlady came in and shouted, 'It's my Birthday.'

"Suddenly there was a lock in. Free bar, grub and entertainment.

"It was fabulous. Something I will never forget".

While Gareth was working on the site a big white van arrived from which two blokes got out

One approached Gareth and asked him if he would like to buy a colour television set.

"I told him I wasn't interested because I already had one but the site foreman and one of the labourers showed a bit of interest in the televisions which were £50 each.

"I could sense that the TVs were so hot that you could burn your hands on them.

But they handed over the cash.

"With the deal done one of the chaps in the van said they would be back the following day with more TVs and drove off.

"The TVs had bubble wrap around them and when it was removed there were just empty TV sets with bricks inside them.

"What a scam that turned out to be."

Gareth said that it didn't end there because on one occasion a smartly dressed man came on to the site claiming he had run out of petrol and was asking people for a loan of £10 to buy fuel.

"I told him straight that I didn't have any money."

Gareth said the same labourer that had been conned with the TV was thinking about handing over a tenner.

"The bloke said that he would give the labourer his card, car keys and his phone as proof he was being legit then took the tenner and off he went never to be seen hide nor hair of again.

"Of course, it turned out that it wasn't his card, the bunch of car keys were useless, and the phone was kaput.

"I was glad to get out of London."

Gareth also remembers a time he had a phone call off a chap called Charles Bassett who lived in Maesycwmmer.

"Anyway, I went to have a look at the roofing job and when I got there, I could see that his back garden was littered with plants and building material.

"When I noticed he had an old bath in the garden of course I had to say to him 'It's a bit exposed having a bath out here in the garden isn't it?'

"With that he burst out laughing and said, 'You've got the job.'

"He was a real gent and used to spoil us rotten while working there."

Another customer will never forget is former Wales, Llanelli and Cardiff rugby player Brian Davies, (pictured) who was capped three times for Wales and following his retirement was a pundit for BBC Radio Wales.

Brian's career started at Stradey Park, Llanelli, near his home village of Llangennech.

He then went on to represent Cardiff, Newbridge and Neath on the first-class circuit before stepping down to help the village sides at Pontyclun initially and then Pentyrch.

Gareth said: "I did a lot of work for Brian at his home in Creigau

"He really was a lovely guy.

"I got very friendly with Brian and his family and because of his contacts he put a lot of work my way."

In 2022 Brian, who later became a revered figure at Pentyrch RFC, died at the age of 79.

Brian is survived by his wife, Enid, daughter Kate and grandchildren.

Of course, there were times when Gareth found it difficult to get payment from a customer, which happened while working on a job in Penarth.

He said: "It was a labour only job, so I put in a price and I did the main roof which I got paid for.

"The owner also wanted me to work on a garage and a sort of long porch which came to a cost of £315.

"I knew he had a bit of a cash problem and when he asked me if I could wait a few weeks for the payment, I said I was okay with it".

The couple of weeks turned into a couple of months with no sign of a payment being made.

"It got to the point that I was calling him on the telephone at 6am on a Sunday reminding him about the outstanding payment.

"So finally, he called me and said he had the £350 payment.

"£350? There was no way I was going to tell him that was an overpayment because he had kept me waiting long enough for it."

A few weeks later Gareth was in an outfitter's shop in Cardiff hiring a "penguin suit" for his daughter Rhiannon's wedding when who should walk in was the much talked about customer from Penarth.

"I gave him a wink and told him it was a good job he paid me but having said that there no hard feelings."

Gareth always maintains that back in the 1980s Pontypridd was the roofing capital of South Wales.

"There were roofers everywhere and during the Miner's Strike they increased tenfold, and they all had coal hammers which are used to crush coal with."

Although Gareth felt he was totally competent doing his roofing work he would always be grateful to Mel Bolderson for teaching him the finer points like measuring and marking out.

Gareth said: "Looking back there were roofing times that I had to cope with extreme weather temperatures.

"I never really lost a lot of work because of bad weather.

"If there was snow on the roof, I would get up there and shovel and brush it off it was as simple as that.

"And of course there was no scaffolding back then."

Gareth also recalled the time when he was working for on a job at the Mornington Meadows site in Caerphilly.

"I was working with a young lad at the time and when we put the ladder up and got on the roof the snow was so thick that when we tried to shovel it off were digging into the felt.

"It was a hopeless task but when I phoned the office to come and pick us up, they weren't happy about it.

Gareth pictured completing roof work on a house in Llandegfedd

"I can recall that one time I was working on a job in Llysworney in the Vale of Glamorgan when I was trying to bed the tile on the verge of the roof and when I was mixing cement in the mixer by the time I got the cement up on to the roof it had frozen solid in the bucket."

Gareth is pictured working on a roof in Llantarnam.

"On another occasion when I was slating a barn conversion in Devon the weather was so hot that I had to take a hosepipe on to the roof and hose the slates down because they were too hot to pick up.

"It was one weather extreme to another."

"The weather conditions were always a risk. I would listen to the weather forecast on the Welsh news.

Gareth said: "With the technical side of roofing, when I learned to measure a roof out it involved the 345 method which is making a big try square.

"Then getting a square line either from the ridge or the eave before working the tiles out accordingly by a gauge stick which was three or four tiles wide.

The finished Llantarnam job with workers.

"Then we'd strike lines with a cement red dye which the line was dipped into.

"When we struck that lane on the felt or the battens the lane would stay there come rain or shine.

"They would be permanent so we could have those lines to work off and by doing that we could virtually do a roof without walking on the tiles".

Gareth also recalled doing a roofing job in a new doctor's surgery in Talbot Green.

"I remember it was a clear day and I had mixed all the cement up and bedded the tiles before going indoors for a break and a sandwich.

"Suddenly the heavens opened up and for about fifteen minutes there was torrential rain.

"I spent the rest of the day washing the roof down, the scaffolding and all the brickwork.

"It was horrendous. I wish I had never gone into work that day."

Another of Gareth's unforgettable roofing memories was when he was working on terraced houses near Bute Street in Cardiff.

"We had two articulated lorries parked on the main road and four of us who were working on the job had to get around 7,000 tiles off the lorries and load them onto the roof.

"We used to race each other while getting the rows of tiles on to the roof.

"Anyway, one of the boys put his bundle into my row by mistake.

"To be fair I told him I would put the bundle back into his row but when I stepped across to do it, I went straight through the roof.

"I somehow managed to hurl the tiles off my shoulder and they went through the ceiling bounced down the stairs before going straight through the glass front door.

"Of course, the plasterers were working on the ceiling and when this happened, they vamoosed pretty quick.

"The upshot was I ended up with a couple of broken ribs but after signing the accident book I got back to working on the roof".

Back in those days Gareth said there weren't the Health and Safety regulations that there are today.

"I never wore a hard hat, but I did wear a Dai cap."

A 1982 memory also gave Gareth some cold comfort when he was living on the Penrhys Estate in the Rhondda.

"It was snowing heavily, and I lived at the top of the site". "I had a Morris Marina car at the time, and I parked it on the top road because I knew I would not be able to get out in the morning to go to work.

"When I got up in the morning the snow had drifted up to my glass front door.

"There was a two-foot gap in the doorway, All the rest was compact snow.

"I pushed my way out and managed to get to my car and I could see that the snow ploughs hadn't been around.

"I hadn't realised that I had left a car window open, only about an inch, but all the snow had blown into the car.

"I had no other option but to leave the car there."

Gareth said that although he was snowed in over the weekend, he needed to get some potatoes so he decided to get hold of the big sledge he had made for his children and go down Penrhys hill to a grocer's shop near the Star pub in Ystrad..

"I whizzed down that hill using the toes of my wellies as brakes.I got to the shop and asked the owner for a bag of potatoes.

He apologised and said he couldn't sell me a bag because he needed to share the potatoes with other customers.

"I told him I wasn't buying a bag of potatoes for myself but I that needed one to share with my Penrhys neighbours.

"He reluctantly sold me a bag of potatoes.

"So, I loaded them on to my sledge and started pulling it up Penrhys Hill.

"I had this horrible feeling that it would take me hours to pull the sledge up to the estate when I spotted a four wheeled drive land rover coming up the hill.

"As he was going, I asked if I could hitch the sledge on to the land rover."

The driver said that Gareth could, but he was not stopping his vehicle.

"He slowed down, and I hitched the sledge on and jumped on the sack of potatoes.

"So, there I was belting up the hill on my hitched-on sledge while those who managed to venture out in the snow couldn't believe what they were seeing.

"Mind you I had a close shave when I came to the roundabout when I nearly came off.

"I really thought I had my chips"

7. "Let's play darts..."

WHEN he was 17 years old Gareth took an interest in playing darts.

He said: "I was working as a van boy with Mother's Pride when a driver gave me a set of darts.

"So, I drew a dart board on the coal house door and just kept practicing on that."

Gareth decided to take his dart playing a step further and visited the Bassett Arms in Pontypridd.

He said: "Back in those days you could only play darts if you marked the board.

"I couldn't mark the board I just didn't have a clue how to do it but to be fair the darters said they would show me, and I would soon get the hang of it which I did and began playing darts on Friday nights.

"I was part of quite a young team, and we won the bottom division of the Pontypridd League".

Gareth said the Bassett team attended a presentation event at Pontypridd Municipal Hall where they were highly praised because they had done so well as a new team.

"It was a very special occasion for the team to get up on the stage and collect the trophies."

Gareth was soon playing around four nights a week, which he really enjoyed not only playing darts but the camaraderie among the players he found to be very special.

Gareth said the major darts tournament back then was the News of the World Darts Championship.

The News of the World Championship was one of the first major organised darts competitions, which began in 1927.

It became England's first national darts competition from 1947, as the years went by it gradually became international essentially becoming the first World Darts Championship and was the hardest darts tournament to win until its demise in 1990.

There was also a brief revival of the event in 1996/97, but it is now discontinued.

Rhondda born darts player Alan Evans became runner up in 1971 while Ynysybwl's Leighton Rees also became runner up 1975.

Leighton Rees pictured with the Farmers Arms A Ladies Team which won the Porth and District Ladies Darts League.

Gareth said: "To get an entry into the News of the World Championship you had to be the tops in darts in your pub then the Pontypridd finals, which were held over two nights because there were so many pubs involved.

"After that there were the County finals and the Welsh finals before the Grand Final was held in Alexander Palace in London.

"We all went up there in 1975 when Leighton Rees (pictured) was in the final.

"Unfortunately, he was beaten 2-0 by Manchester darts player Bill Lennard.

"We all had Watneys Party Sevens beer when we arrived at Crystal Palace and after we had swigged them, we stood on the empties to be able to watch the final because the place was so crowded.

"Of course, we were all rooting for Leighton and were disappointed with the result.

"But to be fair Bill Lennard was the better player on the night".

Leighton, who passed away in 2003 aged 63, is best known as the first BDO World Professional Darts Champion, having won the inaugural 1978 BDO World Darts Championship and was a former World No. 1 player. He was one of the sport's most successful players throughout the 1970s and retired from the game in 1991.

Gareth said: "Leighton was a lovely guy and a top darts player.

"When he won the Embassy, the cash prize was £3,000 which wasn't to be scoffed at.

"I suppose you could buy a house for that back then."

Gareth also recalled the time when he was living on the Penrhys estate in the Rhondda when he went to the Penrhys pub to mark the dartboard and have a game.

"I couldn't believe it when none of the players would loan me their darts.

"So, I took the short trip home got my darts went back to the pub and played and beat them all.

"And of course after that they wanted me to play in their team in the Rhondda League.

"There were eventually three teams which won the division which meant there was a play-off which was 1,001 with a double start at six a side.

"I was the lead man to get a double and start us going and the first two games I started with throws of 156 which really won us the game because that had put us so far in front.

"We won that game, and the next one was a game of Shanghai and it was 10 pence a player so I ended up with a pocketful of 10 pence coins.

"In the end I thought I would give them a break, so I sat down had a pint while they carried on with the game."

Gareth said that during his playing years he had hit maximum shots of 180.

"It was quite an achievement back then but when you think about the new generation of darters hitting a 180 is commonplace.

"But I have it on good authority that the dartboards they use for televised events have very thin wires.

"In my shed I have a blade dartboard and years ago the dart boards had round wires but with thinner wires it means the treble twenties and what have you are wider.

"Also, over the years darts have got better.

"When I watch the old News of the World games played years ago on You Tube, they are using Jim Pike brass darts with feathered or cardboard flights."

On his *You Tube Darts News* channel darts player Matthew Edgar investigates if Unicorn dart boards used in television tournaments by the PDC have bigger trebles than other dart boards.

Besides hitting maximums, a nine-dart finish was unheard of years ago.

Gareth said: "The first nine dart finish I heard about happened during a News of the World tournament down at the Bridge pub in Treforest.

"The news of a nine-dart finish spread like wildfire in the darts playing community.

"It was a big talking point at the time."

Gareth admitted that he never achieved a 170 out shot.

"I came very close on numerous occasions."

Darts World magazine was very popular in the 1970s and while reading an issue Gareth decided to enter a Golden Darts competition.

The entry fee was only £3, and the competition was held in Somerton Park, Newport.

Alf Jeffries was a top Welsh darts player who had won the Denmark Open Men's Competition.

"At the time I didn't know anything about Alf when I stepped up to the oche to play him.

"It was the best of three legs, and I won the first leg.

"In the second leg he was going for an out shot.

"He hit two treble twenties and a single twenty and bust.

"I couldn't believe it nor could Alf's wife who was watching the game

"She was furious and let him have it both barrels. I couldn't believe it.

"Alf went on to win the match but that is an occasion I will never forget.

"It was while playing there that I noticed a lot of fans jotting the scores down.

"I asked one why he was doing it and he said he just liked putting the scores down.

"I'll tell you what-that made me feel very important."

Gareth said that one of the benefits of playing darts was improving his mathematics.

"I was hopeless at maths in school.

"I got four out of a hundred in an examination.

"I would put down my name and sit back.

"That was it.

"But to play darts you had to know a lot of combinations needed for an out shot.

"When you are close to winning a leg, you always had it in your head what you needed to score for the next shot and it became instinctive.

"You didn't pause.

"You knew what shot you had to go for."

Another team Gareth played for was in the Tylorstown Con club.

"The one disappointment I had there was playing in the Club and Institute Union (CIU) Singles competition.

"I was the club champion and had reached the stage where I could have been the Rhondda candidate for the Nationals.

"I couldn't believe it when I was disqualified on a technicality.

"The reason being because I was not a full member, only an honorary member.

"I was gutted. I still can't believe it."

The following year Gareth once again reached the final but was beaten by a darter also named Gareth Pugh.

"I wasn't happy about the way the match went.

"The dart board was on an easel and when my opponent pulled his darts out the board was shaking so I had to wait for it to stop which affected my performance.

"Having said that he was the better player and deserved to win."

In 1983, Gareth was in the audience at an unforgettable darts exhibition played in the Tynewydd Labour club in the Rhondda.

The club was the venue for a Rhondda Leader Darts presentation and the special guest at the event was world darts champion Jocky Wilson.

Jocky Wilson

Jocky Wilson who died in 2012 aged 62 was a Scottish professional darts player.

After turning pro in 1979, he quickly rose to the top of the game. He won the World Professional Darts Championship in 1982, then again in 1989.

He was dogged by ill health however and suddenly retired from the game in December 1995.

Wilson, who sadly died in March 2012 at the age of 62, won the British

Professional Championship a record four times between 1981 and 1988. The Rhondda Darts Championship was a popular event way back then with players from all over the valley taking part.

"You Welsh people are wonderful," Jocky told a packed audience.

"It's nice to come to the Rhondda Valley."

"It's a pleasure to be here."

Jocky was more than happy to give an interview after an exhibition match.

However, he asked the photographer to delay taking pictures because of the camera flash.

He then began to get ready to play an exhibition match which the crowd were eager to see.

Barely 20 minutes after giving his speech the wee Scot was swiftly ushered out of the main hall which had erupted into one "hell of a ding dong."

It looked like something out of a cowboy film with fists flying, chairs and tables upturned and shattered glasses everywhere.

Gareth said: "It was incredible.

"There were trophies for the highest out, League winners, scores of 180 and Pub Singles Player of the Year.

"I had my trophies in a crisp box and I just sat there drinking my pint while all hell broke loose around me."

After moving from Penrhys to Hopkinstown Gareth became a darts team member at the Merlin Hotel.

While playing there he was asked to become team captain but said he would do so on one condition.

"I asked them if they wanted to win the League or just enjoy a good night without any pressure.

"They all said they wanted to win the League so in a way I was ruthless. I would only pick who I considered to be the best players, which of course some of them were not too happy about."

After his darts playing time at the Merlin pub Gareth joined a team at Hopkinstown Con Club.

"I fetched a team down from Tylorstown which was really good and then Hopkinstown Con club formed a new team which won the League by 50 points not dropping a leg."

"I was part of a really good Hopkinstown team there.

"We kept winning until we got to the first division where we had our comeuppance and lost a few games".

During his dart playing years Gareth remembers that there were some standout players.

"One is John Madeley who used to play for the Royal Oak, he beat me in the finals of the Pontypridd Singles competition when I first started playing but I got my own back when I beat him in the doubles years later.

"John was a really nice chap and a very good player. He used to partner Leighton Rees on occasions".

There came a time when Gareth knew that his dart team playing days were over.

"I couldn't grip my darts properly.

"It wasn't Dartitis but my fingers began to dry up and I couldn't grip the darts the way I wanted to, so I decided to call it a darts day."

Dartitis is a condition which can affect darts players, and severely damage their performance.

The term is used in reference to players who struggle with some kind of psychological problem with their technique and/or release of their darts.

Gareth said he enjoyed memorable years playing darts.

"They were brilliant times and of course it was great to be part of a winning side but on the other hand you had to accept being beaten and losing gracefully.

"For me there was nothing worse than a bad loser."

8. Hooked on Fishing.

Gareth is pictured in 1983 with a 26lb cod he caught in Swansea Bay.

WHILE a schoolboy living in Thurston Road Gareth first got hooked on fishing.

"During the winter months, especially when there was frost on the roofs my father used to wake me up very early and say, 'come on boy hurry up and get dressed we are going to Cardiff Foreshore'."

Gareth said: "Cardiff Foreshore was very popular at the time because codling, whiting and pouting all used to come into feed there.

"We used to dig our own bait but on this particular occasion we used to fish with frozen herring.

"My dad and I used to have a lot of success on the foreshore while we were there very early in the morning and sometimes at night".

Gareth also recalled the time he and his father went down to Sully Island to dig for ragworm.

The ragworm is highly common on our shores, though rarely seen except by the fishermen that dig them up for bait.

"I'll never forget the time my father got stuck in the sand when the tide was coming in.

"I was panicking and shouting for help to some of the others that were there, and we managed to pull him out of the sand.

"We did manage to get a lot of ragworm which really big and which I called King Ragworm"

King ragworm range in colour from reddish-brown to black and have hundreds of small legs (parapodia) running down the side of their body which are usually yellowish in colour.

They are armed with pincers that are capable of giving a painful nip to an unwary angler.

"While fishing down Cardiff Foreshore sometimes people would go around scrounging bait.

"We knew this was going on so what we used to do is fold the ragworm up in damp newspaper so they would stay alive and fresh when we went fishing.

"On one occasion this big chap came up to us doing his best to scrounge some bait.

"My father told him to help himself to the bait wrapped in the damp newspaper.

"When he picked one up and took the newspaper off, he quickly dropped the bait gave out a hell of a scream and ran off."

There was also the time when Gareth went on holiday to Saundersfoot for some sea fishing.

"We set off around midnight we were fishing off the cliff by the side of the roadway and were using very big cockles for bait which we dug up because there were a lot around at that time.

"I had one of the cockles on my fishing and hook and after casting out I managed to pull in a bass weighing five pounds.

"I was only thirteen years old at the time and I was so thrilled about catching that bass.

"My father went to unhook it, and the bass's back dorsal fin sprang up and spiked him in the hand, so I was a bit wary of them after that."

Years later Gareth and his son, also called Gareth, used to fish off the South Wales coast.

"To be honest the fishing wasn't getting any better there but anyway I bought Gareth a fly rod.

"Then I thought I would also try it.

"We went over to Hopkinstown Cricket Club where a pal called Gary Lewis taught us how to cast a fly rod.

"It wasn't as difficult as I thought it would be and I soon got hooked."

"I have some great memories of fly fishing.

"I got to know where the fish were laying and rising.

"I was never stuck in one spot. I was always on the move."

"People seem to think that fishermen sit on a riverbank and either read a book or fall asleep but that is not the case."

Llyn Clywedog

Gareth also did a lot of fly fishing in Llyn Clywedog in Powys.

The Llyn Clywedog is a man-made reservoir formed by the construction of the Clywedog Dam. The lake has a surface area of 615 acres (230 football pitches), is 216 fee4t deep at its maximum depth and stretches in all a distance of some six miles.

The nearest town was Llanidloes and Gareth got to know Eileen the landlady of a pub called The Red Lion.

"I made her a very large bowl out of Yew. She always gave me a lovely welcome."

"When I was a member of the Rhondda Sea Anglers we used to meet once a fortnight in the Gelligaled pub in Ystrad.

"I'll never forget the time we went there, and they had their raffle you know their local raffle and the prize consisted of a Sunday dinner.

"People were buying the tickets and it came to pass that an elderly woman had won the raffle.

"They presented her with a sack with potatoes and veg in it and also, would you believe, a live chicken.

"The chicken got out of the sack and was running around the pub.

"I couldn't believe what I was seeing."

Gareth also used to fish locally in the River Rhondda and the River Taff.

"A lot of people ask, 'Why go fishing? but for me, and I suppose a lot of other fishermen the thrill is the challenge not the actual take."

When he got older Gareth had a motorcycle and one night in the Bassett Arms with a pal called Roy Davies, he decided to travel to Thurso in Scotland to see his brother Gwyn who was working up there.

"I had a Triumph Daytona 500 Roy had a BSA Spitfire 650 but there was a problem because his bike would not charge the alternator so every hundred miles or so we had to stop and change over batteries.

"We used to take it in turns to lead and anyway he was in front of me on the motorway when I noticed the exhaust pipe on his bike was dropping down.

"I quickly changed to the inside lane tried to signal to him about the exhaust dropping down.

"Anyway, eventually his exhaust came off and he pulled over to the side of the motorway.

"I couldn't believe what happened next because Roy decided to walk down the motorway to retrieve his exhaust.

"Cars were whizzing around everywhere and Roy was running and dodging his way on the motorway trying to pick the exhaust up.

"When he finally picked up the exhaust, he burnt his hand because it was so and let out one hell of a scream.

"I was in hysterics. I couldn't stop laughing."

The pair of them managed to cut some wire fencing and somehow get the exhaust back on the bike.

Eventually Gareth and Roy got to the top moors on the A9 road at the top of Scotland in a thick fog about one o'clock in the morning.

Gareth said: "I was leading and when I looked ahead, I could see all these green lights and for some reason I just jammed on the brakes.

"We both stopped because there was a herd of what looked like some sort of deer, and we were lucky we didn't run into them".

Gareth and Roy eventually arrive in Thurso around two o'clock in the morning.

"It took us 22 hours to get to Thurso because I don't know how many times we stopped to smoke a fag.

"I had trouble finding my brother's address but in the middle of the town there was a map board which you could press a button for a map to light up to show where you were located.

"That map board was brilliant because it pinpointed my brother's address."

It was then that Gareth began to have problems with his motorbike exhaust which was spewing out blue and green flame and sounding like a military tank.

"There I was riding on the pavements looking for my brother's address and every house I passed I could see the lights being switched on."

At last, they found the house and announced their arrival by waking Gareth's brother up.

"While we were in Thurso I took my bathing costume with me and I thought I'd have a swim in the sea because the sea was very, very, clear.

"I got part way into the sea, and I thought my body had been cut in half because the sea was that cold.

"I quickly came out of the sea and my brother suggested that we go and swim in the River Thurso.

"I decided to give it a go and when I arrived there, I was amazed at the big salmon pools there.

"I dived in amongst the salmon and at first it was a little bit unnerving but then I felt it to be thrilling because I was swimming with these massive salmon.

"It really was enjoyable.

"That trip was quite an experience, and I have to say the Scottish people were wonderful."

So, it was now time to return home which Gareth described as a "hard drive back."

"On the drive back around about midnight the weather turned nasty and with hailstones falling so we decided to stop under a motorway bridge. Suddenly a police car pulls up and a copper steps out and said, 'what are you pair doing here?'

"We told him we were sheltering because the bad weather made it too dangerous to carry on.

"He told us to move on, but we ignored him and waited for the weather to improve before carrying on with our journey.

"While we were waiting there this lad pulls up on a small motorbike and after greeting him, I asked him where he was going?

"France," he replied.

"He asked us if we would like something to eat and of course we were both starving and with that he opened up one of the panniers on his motor bike and pulled out a French loaf and what have you."

The newcomer then asked Gareth and Roy where they planned to stay the night.

"I told him we were going to stop in a motorway services and sleep on a couch."

However, when they did find a services, it was closed. "Not to worry," said the stranger, "I have got a tent."

The three of them rode over some grass and pitched the tent.

Gareth said: "I took my helmet off, laid down and went to sleep as simple as that."

The next morning the weather was good so the three of them got back on the motorway.

"Because this bloke had a small motorbike while we had powerful machines, we held back on our speed but to our amazement he decided ride his bike up and down the banking.

"It was unbelievable, and Roy and I were glad to see the back of him and his motorbike."

With the Scottish ride over Gareth traded in his Triumph Daytona motorbike for a brand-new Triumph Bonneville 750 which cost around £800 from BSA House in Cardiff.

Gareth also has a vivid memory of passing his motorbike test in Treorchy.

He said: "I had the Java CZ back then and I was quite hopeful of passing because I had been told by other bikers that Treorchy was a good place to try your test.

"The only thing that I was worried about was that my speedometer wasn't working properly.

"I met the chap who was assessing me, and he told me to travel up the road at 30 miles per hour.

"So off I went at 30 miles per hour, and everything seemed fine.

"When I went around the block and came back to the examiner, he gave me a route to follow and told me that somewhere along the way he was going to step out in front of me and test me for an emergency stop.

"Anyway, while I was travelling along the route he jumped in front of me so I slammed on my brakes.

"I stopped in time but I stalled the bike, so I turned to the examiner if he didn't mind me bump starting the bike.

"He gave a long sigh and said..'Oh go on then.'

"So, I bump started the bike and finished the test."

The examiner then asked Gareth a couple of questions before handing him a form which he didn't even look at.

"I saw one of my mates who asked me if I had passed the test, and I told him no.

"He asked to look at the form and when I took it out of my pocket, I couldn't believe that I had passed.

"The examiner didn't tell me I had passed so I thought I must have failed."

9. The African Trip.

THE late 1990s proved to be not a good time in Gareth's life.

His father died, he was made redundant from his job with Mel Bolderson and his marriage collapsed.

"My brother Gwyn got in touch and suggested that I visit him out in Zambia to spend some time out there with him."

Gwyn's job in Zambia was teaching local people how to fabricate fitting welding.

Gareth said: "Gwyn was proficient in stain steel welding while living in Scotland so it was just the job for him.

"It was nice of Gwyn to make me an offer to join him in Zambia, but I told him there was no way I could make the trip because I just couldn't afford it.

"But he said not to worry that he would finance it."

So that was it.

Gareth set off for Heathrow airport and boarded a flight to Zambia on a Jumbo 747.

"It was quite an experience for me because I had never been on a Jumbo 747."

Gareth eventually arrived at Lusaka airport which is the largest airport in Zambia.

"From Lusaka I boarded a small plain to go out into the bush to a place called Kitwe."

Kitwe, city situated in northern Zambia is the second largest city in Zambia and is the main industrial and commercial centre of the copper-belt region.

"When I stepped off the flight, I had this feeling that I looked ridiculously out of place because I the clothes on that I would be walking around Pontypridd on an Autumn day while everyone was walking around in shorts.

"The heat was intense.

"I never felt anything like it".

Gareth was quite relieved to arrive at his brother's home, which he described as "a type of villa".

"I was amazed. Gwyn had employed housemaids, guards and gardeners and he also had two Rhodesian Ridgeback dogs."

The Rhodesian Ridgeback is a large dog breed bred in the Southern Africa region.

Its forebears can be traced to the semi-domesticated ridged hunting and guardian dogs of the Khoikhoi.

These were interbred with European dogs by the early colonists of the Cape Colony to assist in the hunting of lions.

On his first night there, Gwyn took Gareth to his local club where Gareth said the beer was not as refined as a pint back in Pontypridd.

While there Gwyn pointed to a large bell on the bar and said to Gareth: "Go on give it a ring."

Gareth gave the bell a ring only to find out that was the signal for drinks all round on him.

"I was totally taken aback but Gwyn gave me a cheeky grin and said he would pay for the drinks, so a good time was had by all."

On one occasion Gwyn took Gareth to a restaurant where he said he was served the finest fish he had ever tasted.

"It was a Nile Perch which is caught in Lake Kariba."

Lake Kariba is the world's largest artificial lake and reservoir by volume.

It lies 1,300 kilometres (810 mi) upstream from the Indian Ocean, along the border between Zambia and Zimbabwe.

Gareth's next visit was to a copper mine which was 5,500 feet deep.

"The first 2,000 feet of the descent was by a standard lift which must have held about sixty people and my goodness didn't it half hurtle downward.

"After leaving the lift Gareth along with the others boarded a train to carry on through the copper mine in what were very hot conditions.

"I was astonished that the white people rode in the train while the Zambian natives ran alongside it.

"They were only allowed on the train if there was room for them".

The train then took everyone to the next lift shaft but while doing so two sections of rail track needed to be removed and then put in the lift shaft while everyone was in there.

Gareth said: "This action was taken to stop any trains going along the railway line and plunging down the lift shaft while the lift was at the bottom.

"It needed to be done because of a similar incident happening in another copper mine months earlier with the loss of many lives."

Gareth said this lift shaft was more than 2,000 feet and dropped a lot faster than the first one.

"When we got to the bottom of this lift there were tunnels leading off everywhere.

"I couldn't get over the huge holes everywhere.

"If anyone stepped in could end up being a life-or-death situation.

Gareth said he would never forget the guide screaming and yelling at the natives who were twice the size of him and who were using big and very powerful drills into the rock.

"There was a lot of machinery down there which they couldn't leave in the tunnels because the compression down there would jam them".

Gareth said the last 900 feet he went down the shift was in a kibble, which is a type of bucket.

"It was quite an experience for me because just stepping into it was a challenge".

When Gareth arrived back up to the surface all he was wearing were overalls, underpants and wellies.

He said:" I was absolutely soaking".

Looking back Gareth said he would never forget that Copper Mining trip which he said was "fascinating."

With the Copper Mining trip over Gareth's next venture was in the Zambian Bush where a white settler was looking after captured wild chimpanzees.

"To look at these chimpanzees up close was very frightening.

"This chap also had peacocks and whenever they passed the cages the chimpanzees would reach out and pull their herls (feathers) out.

"So I asked him if I could have some peacock herls for fly tying while fishing which he kindly gave me quite a few of them.

"He also lived quite near the Zambezi River so without giving it another thought I walked down to the river to have a look around.

"So, after a while I decided to walk back and when I got there one chap asked where I had been.

"So, after I told him he asked, 'did you see any crocodiles?"

"Crocodiles?"

The Zambezi River is one of Africa's most iconic rivers and is home to a wide variety of wildlife.

Crocodiles are one of the river's most feared residents and are known to attack and kill people.

Gareth said: "I shudder to think how stupid I was."

Gareth recalled that the chimpanzee keeper also had a hippopotamus which was a kind of pet.

Every day the hippo used to go into a shed that was so narrow that he barely fitted in there.

"Of course, I wasn't aware of this when I went into the shed.

"But I soon realised that if the hippo decided to move from side to side, he would have squashed me."

"So anyway, when it was time to leave, we gave the keeper a donation to support him looking after the chimpanzees."

The next item on Gareth's African adventure was a barbecue in the local cricket club which he described as being "absolutely run down."

The president of Zambia was Frederick Chiluba. Frederick Jacob Titus Chiluba was a politician who was the second president of Zambia from 1991 to 2002.

Chiluba, a trade union leader, won the country's multi-party presidential election in 1991 as the candidate of the Movement for Multi-party Democracy (MMD), defeating long-time President Kenneth Kaunda.

Gareth said: "I soon became aware of the turmoil that was in Zambia back then."

So, Gareth and Gwyn went down to the cricket club and then went on a long drive to a lake.

"When we got there, we sat at a table which had a straw roof.

"Then the natives would start the barbecue before taking a list of drinks we wanted which they would bring from the cricket club.

"Having got the list they would pick up wheelbarrows and head for the club before returning with the booze and what have you and of course we would pay them because it was the only income they could get."

After a few drinks Gareth needed to go to the toilet and asked his brother where it was.

"Gwyn told me to go over by the lake and do whatever was needed and come back.

"And of course when I came back, he asked me if I saw any crocodiles".

Gareth soon came to realise that the Indians were running the country.

After Zambia achieved independence in 1964, the government started looking to India for material and moral support, and since then the Indian community has played a meaningful role in the Zambian economy.

Most held Zambian or British citizenship with many in professions like banking, retail, farming and mining.

While at the barbecue Gareth said a party of Indians arrived in a big four by four vehicle and with them, they had a brand new ash bin and a massive bag of fruit.

"I couldn't figure out what was happening.

"Two of the natives took the ash bin to the edge of the Bush placed it on the floor before one of them climbed in it.

"He turned the ash bin lid upside down and pulled it over him while the other native piled loads of fruit into the lid.

"Then one of the Indians shouted, 'alright then' and with that some baboons came out of the bush and pounced on the ash bin to have a good old munch of the fruit.

"Suddenly the native inside the ash bin pushed the lid up which made the baboons fall off and faint.

"They may have fainted but the native soon hot footed it away before they came around."

The night before he left Zambia Gareth wanted to have a game of darts so together with Gwyn visited a club to be able to do so.

"There was a dart board there so started practicing and then one of the regulars who was watching me said 'you are not playing with us.'

"Okay so I decided to have a game with the women."

After a while Gareth with a couple of women and some men who he knew decided to go to a night club.

"Gwyn didn't go with us because he wanted to stay behind and play darts".

After a drinking session the group ended up driving to the neighbouring country of Zimbabwe.

They found a house there where they stayed before travelling back to Zambia.

"When I got back to my brother's house he said, 'where the hell have you been?'

When Gareth told him Gwyn said: "I've contacted all the prisons as well as hospitals trying to find you".

Gareth also recalled a time when he was lying in bed one morning.

"It must have been about 7am when I heard this thudding noise.

"I didn't know what it was, so I trooped into the bathroom and there was Gwyn's housemate washing his clothes which were in the bath and she was stamping on them.

"I was amazed when the clothes came out absolutely sparkling.

"She even ironed his socks and underpants.

"There was also a time when I asked her and the other staff if they would like a cup of tea to which they replied, 'Yes please bwana.'

"So I went ahead and starting making the tea in the china cups.

"While I was doing so, they said 'we can't drink the tea out of those cups bwana'.

"Why not?" I asked

"They then pointed to some plastic cups and said, "we have to use those ones."

"It was dreadful. I couldn't believe it.

"When I spoke to my brother about it, he said it was the custom and they had to be treated that way.

"He said that if any household treated them differently it would cause a problem

With Gareth's African trip over it was time for the flight home.

"It was only when he arrived back home and opened a suitcase of fresh sausages, I found peacock herls in there".

When he took a closer look, he could see round lumps of mud stuck to the herls.

"When I broke the lumps of mud up huge blue wasps came out and started flying around the living room.

"I couldn't believe it."

10. Wood Turning.

BECAUSE Gareth really enjoyed carpentry, he decided to join the Cardiff and District Woodcraft Club.

He said: "My wife Lorraine looked on the internet to find anywhere that I could learn to turn wood.

"She knew that it was something that I always wanted to do.

"There were a few clubs around, but they were quite expensive to join.

"Anyway, we eventually came across one called the Cardiff and District Woodcraft Club."

The Vision 21 Unit have facilities across South East Wales with the aim of providing life-changing opportunities for people with learning disabilities to realise their potential through catering, growing, creating, learning and making initiatives.

Many of these projects are social enterprises that provide training for people with learning disabilities and volunteering opportunities for others.

Gareth said: "The Wood Turners project was very well attended with around 80 members.

"Every Monday night there would be wood turning sessions with on average about 35 people attending".

Wood turning is the craft of using a wood lathe with hand-held tools to cut a shape that is symmetrical around the axis of rotation.

The operator is known as a turner, and the skills needed to use the tools were traditionally known as Turnery.

Items made on the lathe include tool handles, candlesticks, egg cups, knobs, lamps, rolling pins and cylindrical boxes.

Gareth said: "Thursday nights were set aside for wood carving which didn't really interest me because I didn't have the patience to become involved in it".

Gareth said he met some very nice people at wood turning sessions and there was one named Alan Richards (pictured) who sadly passed away in 2019.

Gareth said: "Alan worked in the Royal Mint in Llantrisant before he retired, and he really was a very big influence on me.

"He kindly took me to his house in Tonteg and let me have a go on his lathe

"I remember he said to me..'before you know it you will have a houseful of bowls'.

"If I had a problem with my lathe or my tools, he would be up like a shot to help me".

Gareth said that sadly Alan passed away during Covid and because of the restrictions he was unable to attend his funeral.

"However, Alan had a very good send off with many people paying their respects outside his home.

It was very moving.

"Alan's passing was a big loss to the Woodcraft club and myself."

Eventually the Woodcraft club had to leave the Vision 21 unit, and everyone went their own way.

"A new club was set up in Barry, but I really wasn't interested because I suppose I had learned everything I needed to.

"I was the club's chairman for two years which was difficult because of the challenges of meeting all the Health and Safety criteria."

Gareth had built his own shed at his Pontypridd home which housed a lathe before he had joined the Woodcraft club.

"I have had members from various organisations visit my shed and I am always ready to offer tuition. It is also nice for people to drop into the shed for a coffee and a chat."

Gareth was still working as a roofer when on one job he had what turned out to be quite a nasty accident.

"I was working on a house on Pontypridd when I fell off the roof.

"It was really bad weather, pouring with rain and the ladder was placed on artificial grass so I couldn't take it off.

"I was working on a kitchen extension, which was only about 15 foot high when the ladder slipped and down I went.

"Anyway, I got up and felt okay but after a while I wasn't feeling all that clever.

"When I fell, I landed on my side which had a big tape measure in the coat pocket.

"So, I phoned my son in law and asked him to come and pick me up and he took me down to the Royal Glamorgan hospital for me to get checked over.

"I sat in the back of my son in law's van and painfully felt every bump in the road we went over".

When they arrived at the hospital Gareth asked his son-in-law to pop into the reception to tell them he was in the van and they would bring out a wheelchair to take him inside.

He couldn't have been more wrong.

"The next thing that happened was a trauma unit coming out and they clamped me up and goodness knows what.

"Eventually they wheeled me in and I was given scans and tests before the outcome resulted in an Elvis Presley situation.

"I was 'All Shook Up'.

"Luckily I ended up being badly bruised.

It could have been a lot worse."

After recovering from his accident Gareth was faced with another dilemma when after going to the toilet, he discovered some colour in his poo.

"As soon as I became aware of it, I knew I needed to see a doctor.

"After the doctor examined me, he told me that he was going to refer me to the Royal Glamorgan hospital for a colonoscopy."

A colonoscopy is a medical procedure that is done to look for cancer, colon polyps or other abnormalities inside your bowel.

Colonoscopy is done using an instrument called a colonoscope (a type of endoscope) which is a long, thin, flexible tube containing a camera and a light.

When inserted into the rectum and gently pushed along the colon, it allows the doctor to see the lining of the whole large bowel.

"Of course, before they did the colonoscopy I only went and asked where they were going to put the camera.

"Up your backside" was the reply.

But Gareth needed to know more.

"That's fine with me as long as it's not an outside broadcast camera."

Which brought some laughs all around.

Gareth said that while the colonoscopy was being done, he could see what was happening on a screen, so he turned to the doctor and said:

"I bet you are a dab hand at computer games.

"I know it was a serious procedure, but I brought a lot of smiles from those present."

When the procedure was over, cancer was detected at the bottom of Gareth's colon.

Within a week, Gareth was hospitalised when the COVID outbreak had just started.

"Because of the COVID restrictions, I was the only one in the ward I was in.

"There were three nurses just looking after me, and I was spoilt rotten."

Gareth underwent an operation, and when he came back on the ward, he sensed something was wrong, but he couldn't figure out what it was.

"Anyway, I pressed a buzzer, and a nurse came in and took one look at me before saying, 'Look at the mess you have made'.

"What had happened was that the needle had come out of my arm, resulting in blood being everywhere.

"I have to say the nurses who cared for me were brilliant.

"They put me at ease, and I can't speak too highly of them.

"The downside was that I could not have any visitors, which I could understand why.

"When I left the hospital, 35 people went into the ward I was in during the COVID outbreak."

When Gareth was finally discharged from the hospital, he decided to retire.

"I knew it was time to pack in my roofing work.

"I was sixty-six years old, and after all, I had been doing it for almost 50 years."

Gareth said although there were ups and downs during his roofing years there were funny sides which he will never forget.

"I remember one time I was painting the interior of Hopkinstown Church.

"The scaffolders had put staging up for me to paint the arches inside the church.

"The arches were of different colours and while I was doing it, I could hear a slight noise from behind me.

"One of the scaffolders was on his hands and knees crawling towards me on the scaffold to try and scare me.

"I didn't let on that I had seen him.

"I got down off the scaffolding and went behind the church organ.

"Don't ask me why but I had to have this black ski mask on me.

"So, I put the ski mask on and when he came around a pillar looking for me, I quietly crept up behind him and stood up while doing a bit of heavy breathing.

"When he turned around and saw me, he gave a scream I will never forget.

"He thought he could play a prank on me, but I turned the tables."

On another occasion Gareth was working on the roof of a funeral directors when he asked one of his workmates to go down to the back yard and get a bucket of cement.

"There were two storeys on the front of the house and three stores at the back which went down to the back yard.

"At the bottom of the scaffolding at the back there was an entrance.

"So he went down the ladder at the front went through the house and down some narrow stairs to a sort of cellar on the ground floor.

"It was very dark down into the cellar which was sort of a storage space for coffins.

"The switch to turn on the light was behind a curtain in a little alcove.

"And of course typical of me I slid down a scaffolding pole and got there before him and went and hid behind the curtain.

"When he figured out where the light switch was and put his hand into to switch it on, I gently placed my hand on his.

"In a cellar with coffins in it I almost frightened him to death."

Gareth may have retired but his working life was anything but finished.

"I was particularly busy in my shed during Covid.

"I was making nesting boxes as well as making raffle prizes and Christmas gifts for my neighbours."

Gareth said while working in his shed he used to listen to the radio, particularly Radio Wales.

"One morning Radio Wales broadcast a phone in about bowel cancer.

"So, I made a phone call which was aired, and I mentioned my experience with the illness.

"The message I put out to the listeners about bowel cancer was 'don't lose your life for embarrassment.'

"I acted quickly when I knew something was wrong and I would urge people in that situation to do the same".

Gareth also recalled when he was listening to Wynne Evans presenting a programme on Radio Wales.

Wynne Evans is a Welsh singer, presenter, and actor, known for his role as Gio Compario and latterly himself in the Go.compare insurance adverts on television.

"During the programme a question asked was 'What is the strangest thing you have had in your car.?'

"I could easily answer that. It was a live trout.

"I'd caught it down the river down by the Berw allotments in Pontypridd and I had put it in my pal's pond until I got a fish tank up in my house in Penrhys.

"I managed to get a tank, and I fetched the trout home in a bowl of water in the footwell of the car.

"When I got home, I put the trout in the fish tank and made sure everything was working alright.

"My children decided to call the trout Henry.

"A few days later I got up for work and I discovered that Henry was upside down in the fish tank.

"He had snuffed it.

"So, I got it out cleaned and gutted it and put it into the fridge ready for my food when I came home from work.

"When I arrived home looked in the fridge and there was no sign of the trout.

"The kids had only gone and buried it in the garden.".

Gareth was making sure of keeping very active in his retirement.

"No way was I going to sit on a couch in the house and watch TV all day.

That isn't my style."

It was then that Gareth heard from a pal about a locally based Men's Shed organisation. Men's Shed is a community-based project, where men can come together to learn, share skills and make long-lasting friendships together.

The Men's Shed movement was first founded in Australia in the 1980s, and have since expanded to other countries including Ireland, the UK, America, Canada, Iceland and Estonia to name a few.

"Anyway, the Men's Shed organisation caught my interest and I decided to join a Shed which was based in Treforest and I hadn't been there very long before I was made chairman.

"I didn't really want the post, but I took it on to help others.

Gareth demonstrating his fishing skills at the Pontypridd Men's Shed.

"The Men's Shed has been a benefit to me particularly with my wife passing away. I have had outstanding support not only from the Men's Shed members but also friends."

Pontypridd Men's Shed members.
Bob Scott and Dave Mainwaring in Gareth's shed.

While a member of the Men's shed Gareth was asked by Pontypridd Town Council representative Mike Oliver if he could make some bird nesting boxes.

"I told him of course I would, and I did a load of them.

"I think it was 25 for Pontypridd Town Council and more than 20 for the junior schools.

"I felt good to do something for the community."

"I also did some for the Men's Shed which we went and placed on the mountain".

Gareth with his bird nesting boxes.

Gareth has been a member of the Pontypridd based Buffs (The Royal Antediluvian Order of Buffaloes) for more than 20 years.

The Royal Antediluvian Order of Buffaloes (RAOB) is one of the largest fraternal movements in the United Kingdom. The order started in 1822 and has since spread throughout the former British Empire and elsewhere in the world.

It is known as the "Buffs" to members.

Buffalo Lodges functioned as a means of raising funds to help sick and indigent members, their families, and dependents of former members.

Charity has always been at the heart of the Buffaloes and as the movement grew so did the benevolent aspirations culminating in the establishment of orphanages and convalescent homes.

The Buffs are regarded as charitable organisations.

Gareth said: "Sadly the Buffs organisation is diminishing and personally I can't see it continuing".

Another of Gareth's regular activities is bowls.

"My involvement in bowls started when I went to the indoor bowls centre in Pontypridd when a roll up was taking place".

A bowls roll up is a warm up end, without scoring, to enable players to test their bowls in the conditions before a game starts.

Gareth is pictured far left in the middle row with the Pontypridd Bowls Club members and special guest Pontypridd MP Alex Davies-Jones.

"I soon got to grips with that and before long I was asked to join the Pontypridd Bowls Club in Ynysyngharad Park where once again I made some very good friends.

"The Bowls Club is doing very well.

"The year 1924 is a special one because it will be our Centenary Year".

Gareth still goes swimming regularly at the Pontypridd Lido as well travelling to Mid Wales to do fly fishing.

"I want to make the most of my life, it is as simple as that and my advice to anyone who finds themselves struggling with retirement is to find a hobby or something to look forward to.

"I may not have fulfilled my boyhood dream to join a circus and become a clown, but I sure have had a lot of laughs along life's way."

Acknowledgements.

Writing this book would not have been possible without the help of my Pontypridd Men's Shed pal and retired journalist Dave Edwards.

I would also like to offer my thanks to my son Gareth of Pontypridd based Plaingraffic Design Solutions for his support.

I am also indebted to Dianne Gage for her contribution.

Also, to Chris Jones for his help in publishing the book and finally my good fishing pals Jeffrey Szarun, Anthony Camm and Alan Banwell.

During my working years as a roofer, I met many customers who I am delighted to say have become good friends.

www.ingramcontent.com/pod-product-compliance
Lightning Source LLC
Chambersburg PA
CBHW060405050426
42449CB00009B/1912